Wild Homes

Written by Rob Alcraft

Collins

What makes a home?

Wild homes are made with lots of skill!
They help keep living things safe.

Let's take a look.

Dig holes

Rabbits go underground to stay safe.

Families of rabbits dig
holes in the soil.

Make a mound

Termites make steep mounds of soil.

The mound helps their nest stay cool.
A termite mound takes years to make.

Chew!

These insects chew wood into a pulp. They make their smooth, round nest from the pulp.

The queen lays her eggs inside the nest.

Weaving

Weaver birds make nests in the trees by weaving.

Nests made with skill help the bird attract a mate.

Use an old home

Hermit crabs don't make new shells. They use an old shell as a home.

Inside it is safe.

Cut down trees

Beavers cut down trees to make a dam in a river.

Pointed teeth cut the trunks.

Beavers make a home with twigs and logs in the still pool.

Make a web

A cobweb is part home, part trap. Insects collide with the web and get trapped.

The spider waits — then strikes!

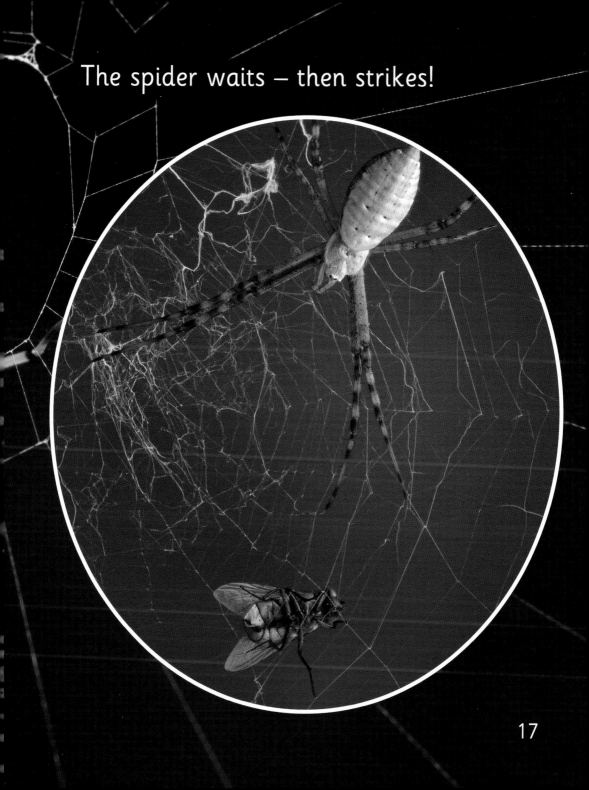

Make a display

Bower birds make their homes to impress a mate.

They seek out items they like.
This bird likes blue!

Home, sweet home!

Some wild homes help living things to stay safe, some trap food and some make a display!

What home?

keeping safe

staying cool

trapping food

making a display

❧ Review: After reading ❧

Use your assessment from hearing the children read to choose any GPCs, words or tricky words that need additional practice.

Read 1: Decoding
- Ask the children to sound talk and blend each of the following words:
  s/m/oo/th   ch/ew   b/l/ue
- Ask the children:
  o Can you tell me which sound is the same in each word? (/oo/)
  o Can you point to the letter or group of letters that represent the /oo/ sound in each word? (*oo, ew, ue*)
  o Can you think of other words that contain the /oo/ sound? (e.g. *zoo, flute*)

Read 2: Prosody
- Choose two double page spreads and model reading with expression to the children. Ask the children to have a go at reading the same pages with expression.
- Show the children how you make the non-fiction text interesting by reading with authority as if you are narrating for a wildlife programme.

Read 3: Comprehension
- Turn to pages 22 and 23 and compare the different benefits of each home from the book.
- For every question ask the children how they know the answer. Ask:
  o How do beavers make their dams? (*cut down trees*)
  o Where does the hermit crab live? (inside a shell)
  o What do you think hermit crabs do when they grow too big to live in one shell? (*they find another one*)
  o Which animal's home did you find most interesting to read about? Why?